WEIRD-BUT-TRUE FACTS ABOUT SCARY THINGS

The Child's World

Published by The Child's World®
1980 Lookout Drive • Mankato, MN 56003-1705
800-599-READ • www.childsworld.com

Acknowledgments
The Child's World®: Mary Berendes, Publishing Director
Red Line Editorial: Editorial direction
The Design Lab: Design
Amnet: Production

ISBN 9781614734161
LCCN 2012946523

Printed in the United States of America
Mankato, MN
November, 2012
PA02143

About the Author

Lauren Coss is a writer and editor who lives in Saint Paul, Minnesota. She loves learning new facts, but she is not afraid of the dark.

About the Illustrator

A former greeting card artist, Mernie Gallagher-Cole is a freelance illustrator with over 28 years experience illustrating for children. Her charming illustrations can be found on greeting cards, party goods, games, puzzles, children's books, and now e-books and educational game apps! She lives in Philadelphia with her husband and two children.

TABLE OF CONTENTS

INTRODUCTION

The world can be a scary place. People have claimed to see ghosts for more than 1,000 years. Cultures all over the world have monster legends. Real monsters might even be living in your own backyard. This book will cover everything from bugs to the boogeyman. And remember, though the facts might seem strange or spooky, they are all true!

CREEPY CRAWLIES

The world's largest spider snacks on birds.

The goliath spider of South America is the size of a dinner plate. It has been known to eat small birds, as well as small animals and reptiles.

The giant centipede of the Amazon can be more than 1 foot (.3 m) long.

This big bug eats almost anything, including bats and lizards.

Some flies hatch in zombie ants.

Phorid flies, a type of South American fly, lay eggs inside of an ant. The baby flies hatch and live inside the ant for weeks. The flies eventually eat the ant's brain and can control the ant's movements.

A cockroach can live for several weeks without its head.

Cockroaches don't bleed, and they breathe through their skin. The body can't eat, but it can move on its own without a head to guide it. In cool conditions, the lonely head can last a few hours.

Some spiders use perfume to trick their prey.

Female moths often have a special scent to attract male moths. Bola spiders make their own version of this scent to trick male moths into coming near them. When the moth gets close, the spider hurls a sticky ball of silk at the moth to capture it.

Zombie rats are attracted to cats.

Some cats have a **parasite** that can be passed on to rats. When a rat unknowingly eats the parasite, the parasite takes over the rat's mind. Soon, the rat wants to be near cats. Usually, the rat ends up becoming a cat's dinner!

For every human on Earth, there are 1.5 billion bugs.

Centipedes are the ultimate track stars.

A 2 inch (5 cm) centipede can move fast enough to travel 4.5 miles per hour (7.2 km/h). For its size, that is equal to a 6 foot (1.8 m) tall human running 160 miles per hour (260 km/h).

MONSTERS AMONG US

A scientist who studies monsters is known as a cryptozoologist.

These scientists search for animals whose existence has not yet been confirmed. The mysterious animals are known as **cryptids**.

People-eating dragons live in Indonesia.

The Komodo dragon can be longer than a car. These animals eat almost anything, including the occasional human. They can run as fast as 11 miles per hour (18 km/h).

In 1909, a monster closed down a city.

According to legend, the Jersey Devil is a mysterious creature that lives in the forests of southern New Jersey. In the span of a week, there were so many reported sightings of the Jersey Devil that schools and factories in Gloucester, New Jersey, were closed.

Lumberjack Albert Ostman claimed a bigfoot family captured him in 1924.

Telling the story in 1954, he recalled that he was taken by the beasts while he was camping in a Canadian forest. The bigfoot family consisted of an adult male and female and a boy and a girl. They held him prisoner for several days before he was able to escape.

Bigfoot needs a shower.

Many people who claim to have sighted bigfoot also report a terrible smell. They say the odor is so strong that it lingers in the air long after the mysterious creature has vanished.

Bigfoot may have had big relatives.

Scientists have found fossils of a giant ape, which they call gigantopithecus. They believe the ape lived more than 300,000 years ago. Its head might have bumped your living room ceiling. Modern bigfoot believers think bigfoot could be a relative of the giant beast.

The Loch Ness Monster was named the most famous Scot in a 2007 survey.

The lake monster beat out famous Scottish writers and actors to earn the number one slot.

In 2009, a man spotted a dark, moving form in a satellite photo on the Internet.

He believed the shape matched descriptions of the legendary Loch Ness Monster.

The Loch Ness Monster legend has been around for more than 1,000 years.

The first reported sighting was in 565 AD. An Irish monk traveling in Scotland claimed to see a large monster in a giant lake.

The most famous image of the Loch Ness Monster is a fake.

Dr. Robert Wilson claimed he photographed the Loch Ness Monster in 1934. Many people believed the grainy image proved the monster's existence. In 1994, Wilson's helper Christian Spurling admitted to the trick on his deathbed.

CREATURES OF THE NIGHT

According to Greek legend, a child born on Christmas Day will turn into a vampire.

▼ Vampires love to count.

Count von Count's love of numbers in Sesame Street has its roots in vampire legend. According to legend, one of the best ways to escape a vampire is to drop small seeds on the ground. The vampire will stay to count each seed while its victim gets away.

It's easier to beat a werewolf than you think.

The werewolf-killing silver bullet is an invention of movies. According to older legends, a werewolf's curse can be broken if someone repeats the monster's human name three times.

There is no boogeyman.

Or is there? Parents around the world come up with different stories about the boogeyman to scare kids into behaving well. But there are no widely agreed-upon features of the boogeyman.

Bob......
Bob....
Bob.....

If you eat puffer fish, you might turn into a zombie.

In Haiti, voodoo priests make a zombie potion with the puffer fish, which includes a **toxin** that damages the brain. When the potion works, the victims become paralyzed, and signs of life disappear. A similar effect has been observed in people who eat badly prepared puffer-fish sushi. This poisonous fish can cause great injury or even death.

Australian kids who misbehave might face a furry, red, frog-octopus man.

Aboriginal Australian kids hear stories of the Yara-ma-yha-who. The monster is said to capture children and drink their blood if they wander into the dangerous Australian Outback.

A fear of night or darkness is known as achluophobia.

Famous scary-movie director Alfred Hitchcock was afraid of eggs.

He had the nerve to direct *The Birds*, in which thousands of birds attack unsuspecting humans, but he could not handle their eggs.

OUT OF THIS WORLD

Project Twinkle was the air force's investigation into mysterious green balls of fire.

The fireballs streaked across the sky over New Mexico from 1948 to 1955. Eventually, the air force ruled the fireballs were actually meteors. But meteor experts didn't agree.

In 1948, two U.S. Air Force pilots reported spotting a glowing, rocket-like ship with rows of windows.

A man on the ground in Georgia had spotted the same craft just an hour before. A few days earlier, witnesses in the Netherlands had reported a similar sighting. The air force decided it was an alien spacecraft, but the report was later rejected. To this day, no one knows what the pilots saw.

UFO or flying pig?

In 1639, Massachusetts Bay Colony governor John Winthrop wrote in his journal that he had seen a bright light above a river near Boston. Eventually, according to Winthrop, the light took the shape of a giant pig.

In 1938, actor Orson Welles gave a radio broadcast that was so scary, listeners believed the world was actually being taken over by aliens.

Based on the book *War of the Worlds*, by H. G. Wells, the broadcast described an alien invasion of a small town in New Jersey.

Many people think crop circles are the work of visiting extraterrestrials.

Some people believe these patterns that form in fields are maps or guides for aliens. However, many human artists admit to creating the patterns using simple tools.

Aliens might do math in fields.

In 2008, a complicated crop circle was discovered in Great Britain. The 150 foot (46 m) wide shape in the field represents the number pi to ten decimal places.

One of the most famous UFO crashes was reported in Roswell, New Mexico, in 1947.

To this day, no one knows for sure what landed near the small desert town. But every year, tens of thousands of people travel to the town for the annual Roswell UFO Festival. It's the biggest UFO Festival in the world.

GHOSTLY GOODIES

One of the most famous gangsters may never have left Alcatraz.

When he was a prisoner in the famous San Francisco, California, prison, Al Capone took up banjo playing. According to stories, people have heard mysterious banjo music coming out of Capone's former cell.

Ghosts aren't always people.

Many people have reported seeing ghostly ships. These ships appear on the horizon and then disappear as suddenly as they came.

Elvis Presley may be the busiest and most famous ghost.

People across the country have reported seeing the King for years. But his favorite place seems to be Graceland, his former home in Tennessee.

First lady Abigail Adams might still be doing laundry in the White House.

Even though Adams died in 1818, people claim to have seen her ghostly figure walking toward the room where she hung her clean sheets to dry. Many people who see Adams also report a smell of clean laundry.

Don't tear up first lady Dolley Madison's garden.

According to legend, President Woodrow Wilson's wife tried to dig up former first lady Madison's rose garden after Wilson took office in 1913. As the story goes, Madison put a stop to it. Even though she had been dead more than 30 years, she was so angry that her ghost scolded the workers to leave her garden as it was. The workers refused to dig it up. The roses in her garden still bloom to this day.

President Abraham Lincoln may still be sleeping in his presidential bedroom.

Many White House visitors and residents have reported seeing Lincoln's ghost wandering the White House halls. British Prime Minister Winston Churchill reportedly refused to sleep in Lincoln's old bedroom after he believed he saw the former president leaning against the fireplace in the room.

A ghost hunter's best tool can be a simple thermometer.

Many people believe cold areas of a room are caused by ghosts. So if you notice the temperature dropping, it might be a sign that a ghostly presence is nearby!

If you record a quiet room, you might catch a ghostly whisper.

Ghost hunters often try to capture electronic voice **phenomena**, or EVPs. Even though the hunters don't hear anything while they are in the room, playing the tape back sometimes reveals new noises or even words. Ghost hunters believe these noises may be voices from beyond the grave.

Is that white spot in your photo a ghost?

Many ghost hunters believe ghosts that aren't visible to the human eye can be seen in photos. The ghost might show up as a small ball of light or a mysterious mist. **Skeptics** say these phenomena are caused by bugs or dust particles.

One of the oldest known ghost stories is 2,000 years old.

Roman writer and politician Pliny the Younger claimed his house was haunted. In letters, he wrote of a ghostly old, bearded man who rattled his chains.

GLOSSARY

cryptids (KRIP-tidz)
Cryptids are animals whose existence has not been proven. Bigfoot is a famous cryptid.

cryptozoologist (KRIP-toh-zoo-ah-luh-jist)
A cryptozoologist studies animals whose existence has not been proven. Cryptozoologists track mysterious cryptids, such as Bigfoot and the Loch Ness monster.

phenomena (fuh-NAH-muh-nah)
Phenomena are facts or events that can be seen or experienced. Some ghost hunters believe electronic voice phenomena are ghosts trying to communicate.

skeptics (SKEP-tikz)
People who doubt or don't believe in something are skeptics. Many skeptics believe ghostly images are caused by particles of dust.

toxin (TAHK-sin)
A toxin is a substance that is very poisonous. A toxin in puffer fish can be dangerous to people.

LEARN MORE

BOOKS

Cox, Greg. *Bigfoot*. New York: Rosen, 2002.

Seymour, Simon. *Animals Nobody Loves*. New York: SeaStar Books, 2001.

Seymour, Simon. *Ghosts*. Mineola, NY: Dover Publications, 2012.

WEB SITES

Visit our Web site for links about weird scary facts: **childsworld.com/links**

Note to Parents, Teachers, and Librarians: We routinely verify our Web links to make sure they are safe and active sites. So encourage your readers to check them out!

INDEX

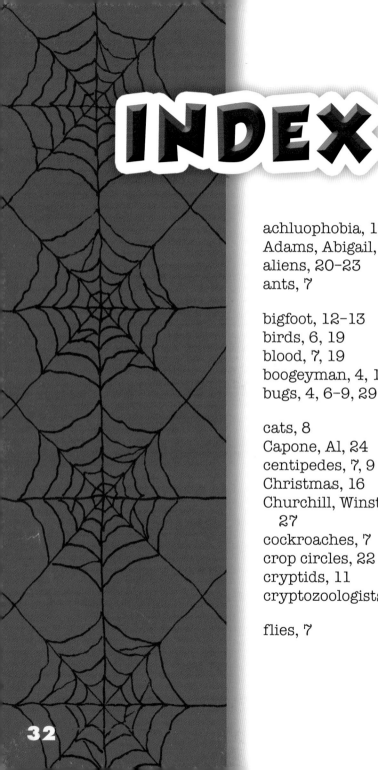